Mental he

What Has Relationship C

Copyright © SUSAN ABRAHAM. All rights reserved.

No part of this book may be reproduced, stored in a retrieval system, or transmitted by any means without the written permission of the author.

ISBN: 9798282605358

Because of the dynamic nature of the Internet, any web addresses or links contained in this book may have changed since publication and may no longer be valid.

The author hereby disclaims any responsibility for them.

To have a good relationship with others, one must first have a good relationship with own self.

Poor relationship to self will result in poor relationship with others because you cannot give what you don't hav

Content

Introduction..6

1. What is Mental Health?.........................9

2. What is relationship?............................15

3. Protect Your Relationship – Protect Your Family..26

4. The Family..36

5. The Community....................................45

6. The School...54

7. The Significant Others.........................61

8. Mental Ill-Health……………………………………70

9. The Most Important Relationship………………80

10. Self Help Tips……………………………………..93

12. Personal Reflection……………………………103

13. Useful Quotes…………………………………....131

Acknowledgement ……………………….…………135

Author's Page…………………………….…………..137

Words Associated with Mental Health / Ill-Health………………………………………….………143

Introduction

There is a lot of open talk about mental health in this twenty first century than ever before. Thanks to some celebrities and royalties who have supported these open discussions and even get the needed help for themselves. Subsequently those struggling especially the young people have open up more to talking about their mental health and to seek for help. Access to help has also been made easy through the Internet and online services, it can just be by a phone call, video call, text message, live chat or email message. The Covid pandemic and lockdown events had further open up access to the whole world for counselling and therapeutic works. It is easy for therapist to work across the world from the comfort of their homes and offices. While clients can connect from different environments which can be their homes, offices and open spaces such as parks, gardens, sea sides and others.

Research has recorded a rise in the number of people seeking for therapy since 2020 than ever in history; the legacy of the pandemic. According to World Health Organisation (WHO) mental health conditions are increasing worldwide. This is caused by increase stress, fear, anxiety, parental depression, negative family environment (may include parental substance abuse, child maltreatment or abuse by parents, loneliness, economic and financial stress, to name but a few). One adult in eight (12.1%) receives mental health treatment with 10.4% receiving medication and 3% receiving psychological therapy.

Compare this to the past where mental health struggle was viewed as shameful, visits to a therapist were kept as a secret and the victims were put in confinement. We have come a long way. However, we still need to evolve. With the current world situation, it is not likely that there will be less mental health problems in the future. The assumption is that it is likely to get worse.

The aim of writing this book is to help open the mind of the reader to the possible causes of mental health problems, ways that it can be prevented and how good mental health can be attained and maintained. The knowledge, help and subsequent freedom of an individual can lead to that of the family, future generations and subsequently to the community and the nation. Let's advocate for good mental health to all. This echoes the theme of 2022's World Mental Health Day, set by the World Federation for Mental Health, 'Make Mental Health and Wellbeing for all a global priority'.

Let's hope reaching out for help with Mental ill-health will parallel the calling for and visiting the doctor for Physical ill-health. And that Mental Health professionals will be able to offer high quality, safe, effective and compassionate help to their patients / clients that will ensure healing and restoration, with subsequent alleviation of suffering.

This is the future I'm aiming for by writing of this book. Let there be no more shame for the mentally ill individual. Rather, let there be compassionate offer of help that the individual can and will be able to access and receive. Let the help offered also bring healing and restoration to the individual's mind and emotion, and release him / her into a healthy lifestyle, identity and destiny.

Let the evolution that has already started be accelerated, achieved and celebrated for the human race.

Chapter 1

What is Mental Health?

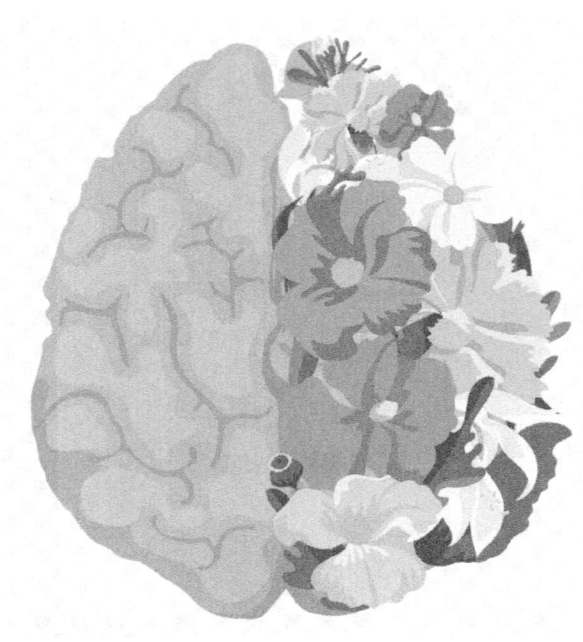

Mental health includes our emotional, cognitive, psychological and social wellbeing and health. It's about being able to think with clarity, have awareness of our feelings, the impact on our choices and actions, and the subsequent effect on our relationships. It also helps determine how we handle stressful situations in our lives.

Mental health is important to all humans and in all ages because as the true saying goes, 'Without Mental Health, there is no Life'. Our ability to live well, right and enjoy our lives depends on our Mental Health. Subsequently, this affects our ability to relate well and enjoy our relationships in our families, communities, work places and other social gatherings.

Let's look at emotional, cognitive, psychological and social wellbeing in detail:

Emotional wellbeing:

This is about our feelings. How we feel when we face certain situations or circumstances or people. Every situation we encounter in life will provoke some feelings in us. Some situations will provoke good feelings like peace, joy, happiness. As humans, we express our joy and happiness by smiling, laughing, dancing and cheering or clapping, shouting with excitement and hugging each other.

Peace helps us feel safe and secure and able to love and receive love.

On the other hand, some situations will provoke the negative feelings of sadness, fear, worry and anxiety, or anger. It is equally important to be able to express these feelings appropriately as humans:

Sad feelings by crying.

Fear by retreating, running away or confronting.

Worry and anxiety by exploring what we can do and acting on it

Anger by releasing it in a safe way. Being aware we can hurt the significant people in our lives, we learn to confront issues with love, openness and honesty, and build trust in our relationships.

Emotional wellbeing therefore is being aware of our feelings and having the capacity to express them authentically.

Note; Our feelings are part of what makes us humans. We don't need to shy away, suppressed or be ashamed of them. We just need to acknowledge, accept and expressed them appropriately.

Cognitive wellbeing:

This is about our thoughts. The ability to think clearly and reason properly without confusion or distortion. Subsequently this affects our choices and consequently our actions. The outcome of clarity in thinking will always lead to finding purpose, meaning and fulfilment in life and the ability to progress, be successful and happy.

Psychological wellbeing:

This is the combination of emotional and cognitive wellbeing which are inter-related. Our thoughts affect our feelings and vice versa. So, when we face a situation, immediately our feelings become provoke. This can just be spontaneous because our feelings are controlled by our Autonomous Nervous System. Or based on what we think about that situation when the information gets into the cognitive part of our brain, the frontal lobe. Our ability to process both feelings and thoughts properly will result in making the right choices and decisions or in taking the right actions. This facilitates the ability of the individual to self-regulate and function normally in day-to-day activities of living.

Social wellbeing:

This is about our relationship with others. We are social beings as well as individuals. None of us can thrive in a vacuum. We need others in our lives. The ability to relate with others in healthy social settings enhance our overall health and the ability to thrive and be successful and happy in life. It has been recognised in health care that many patients who visit the doctors and hospitals frequently are struggling with their social lives. As such, a team of workers called Social Prescribers have been employed to support these individuals. And there has been life changing feedbacks from those who have accessed these services.

Summary: Human beings are complex beings. There is a whole lot to our lives than the physical. Most times, we pay more attention to our physical bodies and outlook. However, the non-physical which are our emotions and thoughts are very important and needs our utmost attention and care. Most of the problems we have in our physical bodies are outcome of the state of our psychological health. These are called psychosomatic illnesses. The only way these illnesses are resolved is when the psychological problems are addressed and resolved. This is an indication that shows how important our Mental Health is. Let's pay attention to our mental health so we can have healthy lives and relationships, healthy families and communities, and subsequently healthy nations. This is what would make our world a better place.

Chapter 2

What is Relationship?

The Oxford Dictionary described relationship as the way in which two or more people or things are connected, or the state of being connected.

The purpose of this book is to look at human relationships.

The onset of the human relationship:

Many people will have different ideas and opinions about when the human relationships start. Studies have shown that the unborn baby is affected by the mother's mood. Stress, depression and anxiety during pregnancy can mean a higher risk of offspring developing ADHD, depression or other conditions. Bearing this in mind, I believe the human relationship starts from the womb, that is, from conception. The first relationship for a baby is while in the womb. Mothers can relate with having an awakening to love once they missed their period and know they are pregnant unless in exceptional circumstances. Then as the pregnancy progressed, the baby can feel the mother's touch and can hear her voice and can respond to it. Studies have also shown the baby can hear the father's voice and respond to it. There is information on the Internet advising men of what to say or not say to their pregnant wives to ensure their emotional and mental wellbeing, and subsequently that of the unborn baby. Men need to take advantage of these information because raising healthy kids begin right at conception. It is not just about the mother; the father is an important part of this relationship.

Here's some tips on how men should support their wives /partners:

During pregnancy:

- Be present – at appointments, shopping for essentials and classes.
- Support and positively acknowledge the changes her body is going through.
- Make healthy lifestyle changes for yourself. If you smoke, work on quitting; if you are overweight, improve your diet and exercise routine; if you have mental health problems or an addiction, work on

them and get the support and help you need. You need to be the best you can for your partner and your child.

- Make her comfortable. Massages, foot and leg rubs, a warm bath, extra pillows – all of these things make pregnant bodies more comfortable.

- Learn as much as you can and support her in her birthing options.

- Seize the moment. This is literally the last few months you have together alone. Have fun, travel, enjoy intimate times.

During labour and delivery:

- Provide distractions. Bring her favourite DVD series, turn on the music, give her a back rub. All of these things can improve her tolerance to labour.

- Be her advocate. She may not be able to recall what she wants when she is "in the moment." Be a calming presence and voice for her when she needs it.

- Expect and humour a bit of frustration from her. She is exhausted, she is uncomfortable and she may be easily annoyed.

- Take pictures and videos. You will both forget a lot the first few days, and it's nice to have a way to remember the moments.

After delivery:

- Allow yourselves a chance to debrief. Talk about the experience and your baby.
- Become an expert diaper changer and bath giver.
- Rock your baby to sleep so mom can rest after nursing.
- Hold your baby at meals. Your partner needs nourishment and an arm to feed herself.
- Develop routines such as bath or bedtime. This can be a regular break for mom but also a way for you to remain engaged on a regular basis with your little one.

- Understand that emotions may run high. Support her, tell her that she is doing a good job as a mother; make her feel loved.
- Take on parts of cooking, cleaning or household tasks she may feel responsible for. Let her know you care by doing things without being asked.
- Ask her what she needs from you. She may not offer this up otherwise.
- Take care of your basic needs so you can be the rested one during a restless night, the sane one

when everything seems insane, the alert one when the duty calls for it.

So, congratulations and enjoy the journey. You and your partner will make a great team. You are an integral part of her care before, during and after the birth of your baby.

(BMC Pregnancy and Childbirth Journal)

Here is my personal experience to proof relationship starts at conception:

When I was pregnant with my first baby, a month into the pregnancy, I started to experience unusual abdominal and pelvic pains. We visited the hospital for investigations. The obstetrician report was that I had fibroid in my uterus (womb). The pregnancy hormones have also triggered the

growth of this fibroid at a rate faster than the baby. There was actually a little bulge on my lower abdomen which was not normal at this stage of the pregnancy. This growing fibroid was pressing on the nerves on my lower abdomen. This was the cause of this pain. This pain increased in intensity so much that I had to be admitted into the Antenatal ward by the second month of the pregnancy for observation and regular administration of analgesia to control the pain. The pain never gets better but worse, the frequency of morphine administration and other pain relief had to be increased. The obstetricians were concern and advised my husband to give consent for the pregnancy to be terminated as they were afraid my life was in danger. My husband shared this concern with some friends and family members who encouraged him to accept the obstetrician advice.

All this was going on without my knowledge. When the information finally got to me, I responded with, 'There is no way I will allow any doctor to take this baby out of my womb. God put this baby here and only he has the right to take it out'. That was my resolved. I was ready to die with this baby. Where did this love come from towards a baby that I could not even feel or see as at then? This was because a loving relationship had developed between me and this baby at conception. I could not stand the thought of anything that will harm my baby.

From then on, the obstetricians and midwives just kept me in the ward for observation and pain relief administration. On daily rounds the obstetricians will ask me, 'Do you have any bleeding?' My respond was always, 'No'. They had decided because of their stand on the duty of care protocol, if I start to bleed, they will have to carry on with the abortion because of the danger to my life. I did understand their concern and agreed with then.

You may wonder how this ended. So let me continue with the story. About three months into the pregnancy and on one eventful day, the pain was very tormenting. I had the maximum dosage of analgesia but they were not effective at all. By mid-afternoon, I was in so much pain that I could not get of the hospital bed. I could not even use a bedpan to pass urine or go to the toilet. I was miserable. My husband visited in the evening which was the visiting time. Seeing me in this situation provoked him and he did something unusual. He just laid his hand on me and rebuked the pain in Jesus' name! Immediately, the pain left. I was able to sit up and guessed what I needed immediately; going to the toilet. He helped me there. Passing urine has never felt so good. I walked back to my bedside with such relief and peace on my face to the amazement of the ward staff. Prior to this time, they did not know what else to do with me or how to help me. Now, they thought it was my husband presence that made the great difference. And indeed, they were right though they did not understand how he worked the miracle.

I remained pain free for the next two days. That was when the obstetricians decided to discharged me home. As they made this decision, they warned me, 'If the pain comes back, please come straight to the ward for admission'. I responded with, 'Never again, will I have that pain, I will be coming for check-ups though'. They laughed and said, 'Look at this lady, only in the first trimester with fibroid and convinced she will not have the pain again!' I kept my peace because I knew the God who delivered me from that pain will not let me be afflicted again. And that was exactly what happened.

The obstetricians gave me more frequent check-ups than usual though. And they planned for an early admission at 38th weeks of gestation. The reason was for more investigations to be carried out in case there is the chances of the fibroid blocking my lower abdomen and interfering with a normal delivery. I could then be delivered by Caesarean Section. I did appreciate the professionalism and care of these group of obstetricians and complied with it all.

My tummy continued to grow as the baby grew. At twenty weeks of gestation, we went for the first Ultrasound Scan. We were excited to see this little figure swimming inside my tummy and she seems to be waving at us as if she was saying, 'Hello'. Around twenty-six weeks, I could feel her gentle kicks. I will put my hand on my tummy and gently stroke her and she will settle. My husband at times will notice the kicks when we are together and would talk to her. We had the sense that there was some emotional connection between her and us right while she was still in the womb. The onset of relationship. It was quite an interesting journey and experience as the pregnancy progressed to full term.

I was full of energy on the eve of the planned admission; did all my housework, cleaning, cooking and storing the food in the fridge / freezer, and got my bag all packed up and ready. Then I enjoyed the evening with a friend who visited. My husband was at work all day. The labour stated that evening. It was just like little cramps on my lower abdomen. I tried not to let my friend notice but she was a fast one. Around 21:00 pm, as she was leaving our house, she said to me, 'Please call me if it happens tonight'. I smiled and thank her for offering to take us to the hospital in her car as we had no car then. I tried to settle back into bed that night but by 12 midnight, I just could not. I told my husband to call our friend. She was so gracious. She came and took us to the hospital. By 12 noon on the day, we were supposed to be admitted, our baby was born. Phew! That certainly knew was victory! I was exhausted from the long labour and could not recall if I just slept off immediately after. My husband was the one the midwives gave the baby to. He reported a moment of awe holding her in his arms. She looked straight into his eyes and something clicked in him; love and bonding. He began to sing to her and felt she listened. I got to see and hold her when I recovered. The physical union and connection were just too wonderful and hard to describe; my heart was full of joy. The gift of a family is just so unique and the relationship so special.

Some people reading this story may identify with this onset of relationship from conception. Some, however may have had a different experience depending on their circumstances or situations. If you feel upset as you read this story, it's okay to acknowledge and accept the emotion. And get help if you need to because this may lead to your emotional and mental healing. I want to encourage you also not to take the guilt trip into your past. You did what you could in your situation. Do yourself a favour now, forgive yourself and let go of the past. Focus on what is good in your life in this present moment and what you can do to change your life and situation and work on it. This will shift you into the good future that is waiting for you. Meanwhile, chose to make the most of your daily life.

Chapter 3

Protect Your Relationship – Protect Your Family

As a couple counsellor, I have worked with many couples who experienced negative changes in their relationship after the birth of their first baby, and these changes eventually lead to a breakdown in their relationship because they did not know how to resolve them. So, what happened?

The birth of a baby, even when the baby was expected and there was a lot of excitement along the journey also come with some challenges. First, the woman's body has undergone immense hormonal and physical changes in the process of pregnancy and delivery. Feeling tired and exhausted in the early days after delivery is the normal body reaction. Hence, the mother needs more rest than usual in order to recover from the stress and strain of pregnancy and labour.

Meanwhile, the newborn baby is totally dependent on the care of the parents in order to survive and thrive. This demand can be draining in the early days as the baby tries to adjust to life outside the comfort of the womb. The mother naturally would be focus on meeting these needs of the baby. This also would add up to her feeling tired and exhausted at the end of the day. She needs a lot of support and understanding from her husband / partner at this time.

Unfortunately, some men do feel left out. In the counselling room I have heard men voiced words such as,

'Suddenly, I was not important to her anymore'.

'All her focus was on the baby'.

'She's a good mother but I feel she does not need me anymore'.

When men feel this way, they can begin to look for happiness and fulfilment outside their relationship; it could be in people or things and affairs can happen. In some instances, they can still be around working and providing for the family but emotionally absent. This disconnection would not only hurt the relationship but the children as well because the children would absorb the negative emotions that is in and between the parents. Strife, conflict and poor relationship between parents damaged children more emotionally and mentally because these does not create a safe and secure environment for children to grow up in.

An emotionally absent dad does more harm to his children's mental and emotional health than a physically absent dad.

Children need a loving, attuning, safe, secure and emotionally stable atmosphere in the home to grow up healthy emotionally and mentally. This is the reason, I want to encourage couples to nurture, build and care for each other after the birth of their babies. Please recognise how

important this is for you as parents and for your children and their future.

You can nurture your relationship by ensuring you intentionally create time for each other. Yes, keep dating each other! This should be times you set aside regularly just to be with each other, talk about your feelings, desires, aspirations and struggles in an open and honest way. Learn to listen to and hold each other emotionally, grow in your friendship with each other and keep your bond strong. By doing this, you would be enhancing your own well-being, protecting your relationship and protecting your family.

If you have supportive extended family members or friends, please reach out to them and take advantage of their help and support especially when your children are still too young to be left on their own. Investing in your relationship will be worth the effort at the long run.

If you struggle in your relationship, please reach out for help from a professional. It's never too late to rebuild. Consider rebuilding your relationship and the benefits thereafter before breaking up. Breaking up would not only hurt you and your partner but also your children and their future, as well as your subsequent generations. You can overcome your current challenges and leave a better legacy for the rest of your generation.

Check out these websites:
- betterhelp.com
- 5lovelanguages.com
- Verywellmind.com

What babies / children need for good mental health

A baby while in the womb is in a state of just being; no struggle, no striving. All his / her needs are from the mother, and these needs are met regardless of what is going on in the mother's life.

However, at birth, this baby needs to work for a living; breath and eat in order to survive. If he or she cannot do this, death will be the outcome.

These needs are:
1. Physical provision; food, drinks, warmth and cleanliness.
2. Bonding: Need for comfort, affection, closeness, affirmations, valuing and trust.
3. Safety and Certainty: Peaceful, loving, affectionate and secure environment and atmosphere to grow up in. Order, stability and routines are vital to babies and children's mental health and well-being.

And because a baby is totally dependent on the parent or care giver to meet these needs, crying at the initial stage of life is the only language they use to communicate their needs. They cry with hope the adult taking care of them will respond to their needs and accordingly meet them. The adult's responses to their cry begins to inform their expectations and predictions and subsequently, their personality emerges from this attachment relationship to their parents or care givers.

Although there is no perfect parent, however, when a parent / care giver is aware of their baby / children needs and make the effort to meet them or repair any rupture when it occurs, this baby / child will form a secure attachment with his / her parents or care giver. The outcome of this will be good mental health that will enable this baby / child to thrive and flourish in life and in adulthood.

Otherwise, when a baby / child's needs are consistently not met by the parent or care giver, this baby / child will then develop a non-secure attachment with this parent / care giver that will subsequently affect their mental health in adult lives, relationships and ability to thrive and flourish.

In psychology, this non-secure attachment is described as:

1. Avoidant Attachment Style: This individual feel uncomfortable with emotional intimacy and closeness, preferring independence and self-sufficiency, difficulty to trust others.

2. Ambivalent Attachment Style: This individual has a deep desire for intimacy and closeness in relationships but also fear of rejection or abandonment, leading to a pattern of seeking constant reassurance and validation, and may experience significant distress when their needs for connection aren't immediately met.

3. Disorganised Attachment Style: These individuals have inconsistent and unpredictable behaviour in relationships, stemming from experiences of trauma, abuse, or neglect in childhood. As adults, they will struggle to find a balance between the need for closeness and fear of intimacy, leading to difficulties in forming and maintaining relationships.

Note: The first two years of a child's life is very crucial because at this stage, the child only responds to the parents or care giver's emotions, actions and tones of voices as the child is totally dependent on

them. The child's personality emerges from the bonds formed with these attachment figures.

Reflection:

What stories were you told surrounding your birth and early childhood days?

If you want to know more about this attachment needs and impact on your life, check out this website:

Drdansiegel.com

Chapter 4

The Family

The Family is the only relationship we do not chose, we are just born into it. Here, I mean the natural or biological family. You may say adoption is an exceptional case. However, in both, a good start and bonding affects the rest of the individual's life in a positive way. Where the start is dysfunctional, this will affect some part of the individual's life in a negative way.

The family is made up of parents, siblings, grandparents, great grandparents and where applicable, uncles, aunties and cousins etc. The quality of relationship between family members affects an individual's mental and emotional health in a significant way from the early stage of life, and sometimes even into adult hood. It is in the family that we first learn how to relate.

As a counsellor, I'm continually amazed at how dysfunctional relationships in the family comes up in the counselling room as the root of a client's deep emotional and mental distress. At times, it is the interruption of a stable relationship especially in the early years of life that can leave a deep grief that manifest later in life as anxiety, depression and distress.

Now, I want to share a few client stories here to clarify what I have just said. My clients agree for their stories to be shared anonymously. All names used here has been changed to protect the identity of these clients.

Alice was a young lady in her 30's who was referred to me because she was suffering from anxiety and depression and will not even leave her house to go to work for over one year. In the course of the counselling sessions, it emerged she was very afraid of death. This fear was triggered by a recent loss of life through miscarriage. Using a Genogram to explore her family history, she became aware of losing a very close aunty at the age of six and the fear she experienced then was relived in the counselling room. Further work was done that help her release the fear. She was able to overcome her anxiety soon after, started to go out by walking her dog and eventually returned back to work and normal life.

Stanley was a young man in his late twenty's referred because he was suffering from intense anxiety and will not go out of his house for years. The trigger to his anxiety was an attack by some youth one day as he was walking his dog. In exploring his anxiety in counselling, he got the awareness of the first time he was afraid of losing his life or that of a family member, and this was at the age of 10 when he witnesses domestic abuse in the family. Further work was done to help him overcome his fears. Before he finished with his sessions, he was able to go out normally. He even applied for a job, got employed and started working. This was after not working for over six years because of his anxiety.

Sarah was a 40 years old lady, very competent in her work and in a managerial position. She came to see me because she felt undermined by her juniors at work, finds herself reacting and then confused that maybe the situation was not as she thought. On exploring her issue, it took her back to an event at the age of 10 that her family did not handle properly. The pain, anger, shame and frustration with her parents and siblings and the outsiders involved in the event all came out in different sessions. At the end of therapy, she stated she became more at peace with herself and the world. There was improvement in her relationships both at home and at work.

Amina was a 26-year-old lady who came for therapy because she had a break up with her partner and was feeling very anxious and depressed. On working through her issues, it took her back to the age of 6 when her father died. Her father was the closest person in her life. At this young age, she did not know how to process her emotions regarding the loss, and in her community, this was not encouraged. She stuffed this down and just carry on with going to school and making the most of her daily life as any child will do. However, she found herself very angry with her mother and unable to relate with her. We work on this loss and the subsequent feelings of anger with mother. She

found the anxiety and depression lifted by the end of therapy and was back to normal life in her family and at work.

Jane was a 57-year-old lady with history of multiple physical health problems. She was referred to me because she lost a close sister and was still grieving after 2 years and unable to move on. We had several sessions working on her bereavement. However, the shift came for her on one session when she got in touched with the root of her anger at the age of 16 towards an abusive step dad. Working on this in subsequent sessions eventually brought her to a place of release and closure. She was then ready to move on with her life and did.

Anne was a 73-year-old lady referred to me because she lost her husband and unable to get over the grief after one year. We work on bereavement for a while. However, her emotion shifted when she got in touched with her childhood issues. She described it as being deeply unhappy because of poor parenting. Further work on the buried negative emotions eventually brought her to a place of released and closure. Subsequently, her bereavement issues were resolved. She moved on with her life and was able to relate better with the rest family members she still had.

Grace was a 55-year-old lady referred to me because she had reduced confidence and anxiety. After the COVID Pandemic, she was stuck indoors and struggled with her daily routines. In the course of the work, she got in touched with her anger towards her mum who used to punish her as a child even when she was not guilty. Mum used to favour her siblings more than her, and currently, mum was being more dependent on her, and she resented this. She feels stressed with mum's demands and hated it. Further work was done to help her release the suppressed anger, and established assertiveness in her relationship with mum and other family members who contributed to her stress. At the end of therapy, she was able to move on with a new way of living and relating with herself and family members. She described herself as being more at peace with self and family.

Sharon was a 32 years old migrant referred because she had a lot of distress and feelings of low mood and depression, lack motivation and interest in life. She was also estranged from her family. There were quite a lot of issues in life that was making this young lady to feel the way she felt. However, the outstanding was the family estrangement. As we explored the conflict in the family that lead to this estrangement, she got in contact with her anger, shame and hatred. Detangling these feelings in subsequent sessions brought her at the end to a place of release. At the end of therapy, she was very happy with herself, and was engaging in further studies and voluntary activities.

James was a 71-year-old man referred because he was struggling with low mood and anxiety which was triggered by a historical event. As we work together, he got to talk about an uncle's death when he was a teenager. This uncle was very close to him and he was taking on his care when he was on an hospital admission. Becoming aware of his feelings during this event and releasing them was the turning point for him. He was able to move on in life at the end of therapy.

Mabel was a 25-year-old lady referred because she had low mood for a long time. She was also described as having a flat mood and unable to feel emotion. On exploring her issues with her, she got in touched with her anger and resentment towards her parents, especially her dad who was not successful in life, and mum for staying with him. Working on this anger and resentment brought her to a place of release at the end. This young lady also got in touched with her self-hatred because she was like her dad. Further work was done to help her accept herself. She was a different person at the end of therapy. Her emotions came alive in a positive way. She got to love herself, had a better relationship with mum and dad, relating well with her friends, actively applied for and secured the kind of job she was happy to do.

Josh was a 25-year-old young man referred because he complained of social anxiety. On exploring this with him in the sessions, her got to the root of it; his parents divorced when he was 10 years old. Though the parents still loved and cared for him after divorce, his life was greatly impacted by the divorce. We did a further work to detangled the negative emotions he carried after the parental divorce. His anxiety was lifted by the end of therapy.

A true story I once heard is that of a man diagnosed with autism when he was a little boy growing up in a home where his dad was a pastor. He described being abused in his home. Some of the abuse he described was his dad being too stern with disciplining him, having no compassion and not meeting his emotional needs. This relationship with his dad became the root of fear and anxiety in his life. Subsequently, his growing up years and future became adversely affected.

I believe no parent intentionally want to abuse their children. However, some parents do not recognise the stresses, emotional and mental challenges that they have. Inadvertently, they can traumatise their children lives by the way they bring them up. This can become a generational trauma until someone in the family line get to recognise and deal with it. Healing from this is an individual responsibility.

Reflection:

What was it like growing up in your family?

Chapter 5

The Community

There is an adage the African culture that says 'It takes a community to raise a child'. I believe there is some truth in this adage. A child in the process of growth is not only influence by the family but also the community that he or she grows up in. In my culture, it was very easy in my early days to walk into the house of a neighbour, play with the children there and even share their meals. In this way, we formed a relationship that had an impact in one way or the other. I remember one particular benefit I had from that relationship. There was a particular food my mother used to prepare that I did not like. However, our neighbours used to like it. They said my mother prepared it in a special way. So, on the days my mother prepared this meal for dinner, I will go into our neighbours' homes in advance and find out what they are having for dinner. Then when my mother served me my portion, I took it into the neighbour's house that I like what they were having for dinner and exchanged my food with theirs. That way, I did not go hungry because my mother will not prepare a different meal for me but I ended up eating what I wanted to eat.

This experience is not the same with that of my children growing up in the West. Yes, we have neighbours as well, some nasty and some very good. However, the freedom in interaction and relationship is limited even with the best neighbours.

When children can relate freely with others in their community, the following is the benefit:

- They develop the ability to initiate and build relationship outside the family.
- Established rapport and communication skill with others outside the home.
- Develop wisdom in dealing with others, self-protection and self-defence.
- Freedom from social anxiety and fear of people.
- Ability to form teams and relate as a team member to others as they play together.
- Creativity through play and interaction.
- Natural development and growth in social life.

On the other hand, when children experience any kind of racism, bullying or abuse of any kind in their community, their emotional and mental health will be affected in a negative way. And depending on the severity of their situation, they may develop fear when they have to go outside their home initially. When this is not recognised and the child supported appropriately, this may progress to social anxiety, anger issues and eventually antisocial behaviour. This negative progression happens as the child who experiences the situation tries to deal with it in the best way that he / she can, especially, when there is no adult intervention to resolve the situation. The worst outcome to this situation will be that child developing criminal behaviours, committing serious crime at some point in his / her life and ending up in the prison in extreme cases.

Here' some stories to support what I have just said:

Elenore was in college when she became pregnant by her boyfriend. The boyfriend felt he was not ready to be a father and asked Elenore to abort the baby. Elenore was very religious and did not want to. Her boyfriend decided to leave her because she chose to keep the pregnancy. Elenore's father was a deacon in his church. He was very ashamed that his daughter became pregnant outside wedlock and rejected her. Elenore's mother died when she was very young, her father was all she had. However, Elenore was adamant she wants to keep her baby. The only option open for her was to leave the community she had grown up in, that means leaving all her friends and extended family members behind her. She braced herself and left to a city where she got herself a one-bedroom apartment and a job in support care. She got herself settled in this community and began to make new friends. Eventually, she gave birth to her baby boy, and named him Charles. With the support of her new friends and work colleagues she was able to go through the immediate afterbirth challenges and nursed her baby who was also growing rapidly and perfectly. She bonded well with her boy and both had a great relationship.

When Charles was old enough to know some of his friends have dads and would ask Elenore about his dad, she only responded with, 'He's a man who chose to walk away, don't worry about him'. So, they continue living happily together.

One Christmas Eve, Elenore finished work late but she needed to go to the shop to get her boy a present. All Charles wanted was a journal. She got the present, wrote some loving words for him, wrapped it up in the shop and put it in the passenger seat of her car. On her way home, she had a ghastly accident and died on the spot. It was the police who went and broke the sad news to Charles. He was only seven years old. Eventually, Charles was taken to stay with the grandad that he had never met until then. His grandad was not dealing with the grief of losing his daughter well. He projected his grief unto Charles and so was not nice to him. At some point, Charles felt his grandad hated him because in his young mind, he did not understand what his grandad was going through. However, his grandad was the only adult now in his life to care for him. So, he had to endure the difficult relationship, and did what he could as any child will do in order to survive.

He found comfort in exploring his new community as any curious child would. One day, he wondered into a farm. As he sat down in a horse shed to write in his journal, a girl of his age met him. She introduced himself as Becky and invited him to help her feed the horses. As time went on, they develop a close friendship. Charles got to overcome the grief and loneliness of losing his mother, and also the challenges of living with a difficult grandad. He and Becky spent most of their time together, working in the farm, studying and playing in the fields. Charles began to bloom. He was fascinated with animals and sets his mind on tending wounded animals and enjoyed seeing them recover. Unfortunately, at the age of 17, his best friend, Becky developed cancer and died. Charles was very grieved. In dealing with his grief, he turned his heart into studying medicine and doing a lot of research on the cure for cancer. He ended up becoming one of the best doctors in his days. He also got married and raised his own family.

This is the positive impact of a good community on a child. Just imagine what Charles life would have been like if he did not have these good experiences in the community that he was growing up in.

Now, let's look at the next story:

Elaine got pregnant by her boyfriend at the age of 15. Both she and her boyfriend were too young to take care of a baby. Elaine's dad stepped in with compassion and took the baby from her when he was five months old. Elaine's dad raised the baby with his wife, who was

Elaine's step mother. The baby's name was Tom. So, Tom grew up with grandad and step grand mum, he was taken good care of by them. However, the community that Tom grew up in was racist towards him as his colour was different. From the age of five, when Tom started School, he experienced racist abuse verbally from other children and at times from some teachers. His grandad and step grand mum were unable to protect him against these abuses. As time goes on Tom began to defend himself by fighting with some of the children who abused him, and refusing to obey some of the teachers. He felt behind with his studies. He was seen as rebellious and antisocial, no one listened to him or care to offer him help.

His grandad was rather stern with him and applied the old ways of discipline with the hope to correct him. However, by not understanding and supporting him appropriately, things went from bad to worse. As time goes on, Tom grew into an angry young man that was difficult to control. He dropped out of school before sixteen years of age. To make matters worse, his grandad died around the same time. His step grand mum sent him back to his mother because she could not cope with him. His mother at this stage was married to another man and had four more children. Tom was like a stranger in that house, not accepted, love or valued. This made him angrier and more uncontrollable.

At the age of 18, his mother threw him out of the house. He became homeless. A matured lady found him on the street and took him in as her boyfriend because he was good looking. However, Tom was now involved in criminal activities, dealing with drugs, and living the kind of lifestyle that the society will regard as not acceptable. He later was caught by the police, tried in court and sent to jail. His life began to spiral downward from then on. At the age of 50, he was repeatedly in and out of jail, had up to nine children with multiple women, unstable and a liability to the government of his nation. On top of this, he had lots of physical health problems.

In my reflection, I felt Tom's life could have been different if the community he grew up in was kind to him as a child. You may have a different opinion.

Working with Tom was not easy because he had developed very strong defences and finds it extremely difficult to trust others. He was referred by his GP and had no awareness of his need for help at the referral point. He only accepted the referral because he was struggling financially. So, he came to me with a completely different expectation. In the process of the work, he would release his anger and frustrations on me. However, before the end of therapy, he began to have some self-awareness, began to take responsibility for his thoughts and feelings, and began to open up for help with other services as he needed. He began to turn his life around and even get connected to some of his children. Working with him was very rewarding to me.

Reflection:

What were your experiences in the community you grew up in?

Chapter 6

The School

Many teachers do not know the power they have over a child under their care. They can nurture and mould the child into a confidence person with the potential of becoming a successful adult or they can break this child and left them feeling less confidence, anxious, and dysfunctional. A child is a great believer in what the teacher tells them about their abilities and potentials.

Some education system classified children into the more intelligent and less intelligent ones. Can you imagine what it is like for a child to hear always that he / she is intelligent? I imagined his / her self-esteem will certainly by lifted. How about the child who is always told he / she is not intelligent enough? This child self-esteem will certainly be low.

Here's some supported stories:

Alice, at the age of 5 years was excited starting school as any child will be. She was a lively child, loves to play with her friends and always happy. Two years into her school life, her mum noticed something was not right. She was apprehensive going to school and doing her maths homework. She will be in a panic and cries when she needed to do this particular homework, and saying to mum, 'No! I'm not good with maths'. Her mum was always encouraging and helping her. At some point, mum had an opportunity to talk with her teacher. Mum then became aware this teacher was having challenges relating with Alice, the only coloured child in her class. Mum took some actions; first she decided to enrol Alice in an extra maths class that was private. Alice began to flourish and was doing well in maths. Next, she moved her to a different school. Alice was so good and enjoying her maths lessons at this stage so much that she became part of a team of pupils participating in maths squeezes with other schools. Alice began to flourish.

Maria, at 35 was successful solicitor. She came to see me because she was struggling in forming and staying in relationships. Exploring her issues with me lead her back to growing up in a very dysfunctional home where dad was not always there and mum was neglectful emotionally and physically. This unstable childhood relationships made it difficult for her to trust others in her relationship as an adult. She was sceptical always. This instability also exposed her to other traumas in her childhood. In one of the very emotional sessions, I asked what was helpful to her. She responded with a smile, 'One of my teachers always encouraged me. She said to me, 'Maria, you can do something great with your life if you focus on your studies'. This teacher's words of encouragement motivated Maria to focus on and to love studying. And the outcome was she became a confident and successful adult. Further work on the childhood issues brought her to the place of freedom to form new relationships with her authentic self.

Rachel was a highly intelligent and successful lady in a high-ranking company. She came for counselling because she was struggling to form and stay in a romantic relationship. On exploring her issues, childhood adversities came up. At six months of age, her mother abandoned her. Her dad was unable to cope with her and his work, so, he left her with his ageing mother to take care of. Her grandmother depended on the support of her uncles and aunties to care for her. Unfortunately, these uncles and aunties were abusing her emotionally, physically and even sexually. Where she calls home was absolutely an unsafe place to grow up in. School became the only safe haven for her. Her only happy place. She loved and enjoyed learning, and playing with friends. And with supportive and encouraging teachers was able to not only survived but thrived, and eventually became an independent and successful adult.

Stella was referred at the age of 61 years to my service because she was debilitated with anxiety and unable to go out of her house after the Covid lockdown had lifted. She had history of anxiety and depression for a long time but was always coping with her daily living activities until during the lockdown. We worked on exploring her coping mechanisms and the possible root of her anxiety and depression. In one of the sessions, she got an interesting awareness and verbalized it; she feels she is not worthy to live and enjoy life because so many people die during the pandemic. On further exploration to find out where this thought / feeling was coming from, she recalled a teacher in her teenage years who used to tell her she is good for nothing because she was struggling in the subject taught by this teacher. Further work was done to undo this internalized emotional abuse, and she began to enjoy her social life thereafter.

Mabel at 37 was established medical personnel, she loves her job and was celebrated by the patients she helped. She came for therapy because she was struggling with relating to some colleagues at work and also unable to relate romantically. On exploring her issues, childhood difficulties came up. Her parents were repeatedly relocating because of her father's employment. She experienced a lot of difficulties trying to find new friends at every move. She was also bullied at schools and was lonely. Parents were not available to her emotionally; father was preoccupied by his work; mother was unable to get over her grief of losing one of her babies. This little girl at the age of 10 years was lonely, depressed and helpless. She had an older brother who was also bullying her at home. Daily life was very difficult. We got to explore her strength and what helped her to survive daily. She reflected on the support of two teachers who were sensitive to her needs, were affirming her emotionally and encouraging her with her studies. With these teachers, School became her safe place where she felt secured and was able to study, grow and became a successful adult.

In concluding this chapter, I want to say, I can personally identify with the power of having a good relationship with our teachers. I am trained and able to write this book because of the support and encouragement of my teachers. My parents were not educated and as such did not even know how to help with homework and any other school related projects. However, I had teachers who were very supportive and encouraging all through my school life. Some guided me in my career path when I did not know what to do, and motivated me with good counselling when I felt like giving up. I owe my success in life to these teachers.

There are also many children I know and hear of who have prevailed through life adversities and traumas to become successful in life just because of their teachers

The value of good education cannot be underestimated where the future of a child is concern. Above all, the value of a good teacher who take time to listen to, and care for a child who is struggling is priceless. I hope any teacher reading this will be encouraged and keep up the good work – the future of that child in your class depends a lot on you!

Reflection:

What was your school life like?

Chapter 7

Significant Others

Significant others include anyone involve in the life of a child in his / her growing up years. This could be family members, neighbours, friends of the family, fostering parents, care givers in case of looked after children etc, as you can see in this story:

Maxim had a childhood full of adversity and struggles. Raised by a single mum in a country with no social services, her mum was responsible for all of her needs in her growing up years. Mum was not educated and so could not get a decent employment; all she could do was petty trading and labouring jobs in the farm. Her mum was a hard worker though and did well in meeting her needs and that of her two siblings. Her dad was living some distance away with his other family. Maxim used to visit him occasionally, but did not like to live there because the atmosphere was not nice. In her early teenage years, her dad died suddenly. This did not mean much to Maxim as she had no close relationship with dad. Two years later, her mum developed some illness that made her unable to continue working and providing for them. Life became much harder. Maxim became a young carer for mum. At the same time, she began to engage in some petty trading as well in order to meet the need for food. They could barely have enough food to survive daily. A local business man had pity on her and decided to employ her to work for him as a sales girl in his gas station at the age of 12, when Maxim finished from primary school. Maxim accepted the offer with delight and the income from this job provided for their needs.

Maxim's great desire was to go to secondary school. Her older brother, who was studying under scholarship in a university decided to save some of his pocket money to support her at the age of 14. Maxim was over the moon at this brother's kindness and help. She left home and her work at the gas station to the town where she lived with a cousin, as she started in secondary school and continued. She loved studying and was soon making new friends, and was happy. On holidays, she will come home to stay with her mum who was still poorly and take care of her. Life was difficult during the holidays. However, there was a couple with a young family who were her neighbours. Maxim used to spend most of her days in their home, helping with their babies. These neighbours loved and accepted her into their home, and provided her with daily meals, care and protection. They also look after her mum.

Maxim's life continued at this pace till she finished secondary school successfully. Moved on to college where she studied nursing. She achieved her nursing grades after three years, was posted to a local health centre where she got established in her work life. She became a great resource to the community. And also, she was better equipped to care for her mum till she passed away, and her younger sibling. Today, Maxim is an accomplished lady with her own family, and a blessing in her community.

Imagine what Maxim's life would have become if she did not have the support of all these people in her growing and dependent years. Every young life is a seed that needs to be nurtured, watered, supported and protected in their growing process. No child should be written off. They all have the potential to become amazing individuals in their family, community and nation. No child has everything but every child has something to bless the world with. All a child needs are the protection, encouragement and support from those around him / her.

Stella at 28 was an intelligent lady working in a high-profile job. She came for therapy because she had lots of struggles in relating with others at work and as friends, broke up from marriage after one year because she could not stand the man. She tends to burst out in anger at the slightest provocation, found herself swearing at co-workers at time. On exploring her issues, she talks about horrendous childhood abuse, sexually, emotionally and relationally. Father was in prison most times because of drug dealings. She lived with mother and step-father who abused her sexually. Even though she told mother about the abuse, mother did nothing about it. She wanted to be with her father whenever he was out of the prison but he was not available for her. She survived her childhood by living in different relative's houses, some were good but some were also abusive. She described her grandmother as the only safe heaven whenever she was with her. Her grandmother's presence, support and encouragement gave her the strength to face life daily, continue in her education and became who she is today. On exploring her anger issues, she became aware it was related to the men who had abused or were not there for her. Further work helped her to release this anger, experienced peace and able to relate better with others.

Ines at 32 was referred to me by her GP because she was struggling to for the last 5 years since the death of her mother, she was struggling to sleep and lack the energy to get up and go to work. In the sessions with me, Ines narrated very traumatic childhood experiences. Both her parents were addicted to alcohol and drug. From a tender age she had experience continual emotional abuse and neglect. She had witness numerous physical abuses of her mother by her father. Social services got to know of the children condition and stepped in to remove her and her siblings from the family home. They were sent to different foster parents. She was seven years old when she went to live with her foster parent. Unfortunately, they were not nice to her. She described the next six years of her life as being as horrible; she was used for labour in the family and emotionally and mentally abused. Finally, at the age of thirteen, she could not take it anymore. She ran away from the house when her foster mother was out, and went to the police station. Her foster mother went to the police station and accused her of stealing her money. However, the police did not believe her foster mother because they found no money with her. They protected her and would not hand her back to her foster mother. They work with Social Services and sent her into Care. She described being in care as the best time of her life because there was no violent in the care Home. She was able to continue in her education. At the age of 17, she started working and took on the responsibility of supporting her mother and the rest of her siblings. Unfortunately, her mother was not able to sort out her issues and died due to an alcoholic related incident. This was like the last straw that broke Ines heart and lead to her depression. In the sessions with me, she worked through her traumas and griefs. And was able to resume work and continue with her life and support to the rest of her siblings.

As you read these stories, I wonder if you are aware of how resilient a child can be. No matter the adversity around a child, he or she can thrive and grow if there is at least one adult who would believe in that child, be present and supportive emotionally and mentally. If there is no such support in place, this child would be left with the wounds of the traumas and adversities. These become mental ill-health unless someone help the child to process the events and release the negative emotions attached to it. However, if this does not happen to the child, when he or she become an adult, the awareness through her emotions and actions and behaviours would motivate him or her to seek the needed help.

Some adults who are not aware of the impact of their childhood traumas and adversities would continue to hurt especially those in a close relationship with them. Conscientious doctors can treat these ones with medication and also refer them to therapy. Both approaches would surely be effective in restoring the health of the mentally ill. I don't advocate medication only because it does not resolve the underlying issues, it can alleviate the symptoms but the side effects can also compound the problem. Medication alone is like taking analgesia to relieve the pain of appendicitis. Unless the appendicitis is dealt with, the problem will get worse and may become life threatening. I would rather recommend therapy, and medication if it cannot be avoided.

Now, I want to conclude this chapter with an experience I had at a recent Continuous Professional Development CPD) training that I had Online. We did an exercise where we were guided to sit in a comfortable position, close our eyes and imagine a world where someone has no deep connection. If you try this exercise, you would see this person lonely, isolated and maybe unhappy.

Conclusion: The distress of disconnection from others is the primary source of psychological distress which are:

- *Loneliness: Lack of intimacy and closeness*

- Depression: Lack of interpersonal pleasures, sadness at lack of relating, less buffer against psychological stressors, being outside community.
- Anxiety: Being without support
- Interpersonal problems: Inability to connect properly, unsatisfying, lack of assertiveness.
- Psychosis: Internal splitting, lack of support
- Physical health problems

Relational Development Theory: Why do people become disconnected?

- Infants have innate need, and capacity to connect with others
- Where attempts to connect are unsatisfying or painful or abusive or frustrating….
- Infant protect self through developing strategies of disconnection; e.g. mental withdrawal, inauthenticity, aloofness
- Strategies become chronic and automatic, and so deployed in adult life where deeper relatedness is possibility, making relationship and connection difficult and stressful.

(PESI webinar: Working at Relational Depth by Mick Cooper)

The above is the reason therapy / counselling is recommended for people with psychological distress

and relationship problems. In therapy, they can begin to feel safe as they develop trust with the therapist / counsellor and open up to relational connections. Subsequently this will bring healing into their lives and relationships outside therapy

Reflection:

Who were the significant people in your growing up years who made you feel loved, valued and accepted?

Chapter 8

Mental ILL-Health

This chapter is not meant to diagnose mental illness, but to give the reader a common knowledge to recognise what mental ill-health is. I have mentioned briefly in the previous chapter what mental ill-health is but would elaborate on it here. The term mental ill-health is use here intentionally. This is to parallel mental ill-health with physical ill-health, and subsequently promote hope, and reduce the despair and shame that has been attached to mental ill-health for decades. In other words, just as someone with physical ill-health will visit a doctor or hospital and get the needed help, someone with mental ill-health can also visit a doctor, psychologist, counsellor, therapist or mental health practitioner for the needed help. And the earliest the intervention, the better the prospect of recovery. This is very crucial for parents and care giver's ability to recognise this signs and symptoms in the young ones under their care, and subsequently take the necessary steps to get the needed help. A partner can support his / her loved one with mental health issue who lack the insight to realise they need help or that help is available.

Research shows one in four people will experience a mental health issue in any given year. The economic cost of mental health issue is estimated at £74 - 99 billion in a year, and the human cost is incalculable. However, learning more about our mental health and ways to get support can empower people to thrive.

So, here we go:

What is mental ill-health?

A mental ill-health is a disorder diagnosed by a medical professional when there is a significant interference with an individual's cognitive, emotional or social abilities. There are different types of mental ill-health and they occur with varying degrees of severity.

NHS (National Health Service) definition:

A mental illness or mental health disorder is an illness that affects the way people think, feel, behave, or interact with others. There are many types of mental illnesses / health disorders with different signs and symptoms.

What causes mental ill-health?

Research shows a number of factors can cause mental ill-health.

Some examples of these factors include:

Genetic factors:

Having a close family member with a mental illness can increase the risk. However, just because one family member has a mental illness doesn't mean that others will. In fact, others may even learn from the affected member and decide to take care of their mental health and stay healthy.

Adverse childhood environment:

Childhood abuse, trauma, or neglect, social isolation or loneliness, experiencing discrimination and stigma, including racism, social disadvantage, poverty and debt.

Drug and alcohol abuse:

Illicit drug use can trigger a manic episode (bipolar disorder) or an episode of psychosis. Drugs such as cocaine, marijuana and amphetamines can cause paranoia.

Trauma and stress in adulthood:

Ongoing traumatic life events or stress such as social isolation, domestic abuse, relationship breakdown, financial or work problems can increase the risk of mental illness. Traumatic experiences such as living in a war zone can increase the risk of Post Traumatic Stress Disorder (PTSD).

Personality factors:

Some traits such as perfectionism or low self-esteem can increase the risk of depression or anxiety.

Unreasonable and uncontrolled anger:

This causes tremendous emotional and mental damage when it comes especially from a significant person in a close relationship, such as spouse, father, mother or care giver. Children growing up in an abusive relationship even though the abuse is not directed towards them, tend to absorb the negative atmosphere and will experience some level of fear in their lives. This fear if not resolve properly can further develop into anxiety and depression later in life.

I can identify with this – growing up in an environment where the men used to erupt into unreasonable and uncontrolled anger towards their spouses, I did not realise the fear and anxiety in me until later in life, and the root was from what I witnessed at the early stages of my life.

And in my clinic, 50% of the clients I work with yearly with anxiety and depression have the roots in witnessing domestic violence at the early stages of their lives. Here's a few stories:

Andrew at 23 was referred because he had debilitating anxiety. He was not working since the age of 19 because of anxiety. The trigger that caused him to go to his doctor eventually was when he went out for a walk with his dog and was attacked by a group of young people. He was able to run home safely but then suffers from panic attacks and palpitations that made him unable to step out of his house for almost one year. Four sessions into working with Andrew, he recalled an incident when he was 10 years old. In this incident, the first thing was hearing his dad's loud voice shouting at his mum as he was getting ready for school one morning. The next thing was seeing mum pushed down the stairs and falling at the landing. In the therapy room, he got the awareness of his fears that mum was going to die, though mum eventually recovered from the fall and broke off from his dad. He then was living with mum until he grew into adulthood. Getting the awareness of the root of his fear of death set him free from then on. After a few more sessions where we work on his relationship with dad, his anxiety was completely resolved. He then went on to resume job applications, got the job he wanted and started to work again.

Types of mental ill-health

- Anxiety and depression are the most common mental ill-health. Research shows 7.8% of people in Britain meeting the criteria for diagnosis, 4 – 10 % of people in England will experience depression in their life time. In my practice, 70% of clients that I see yearly suffers from mild to moderate anxiety or depression or both.

Other types of mental ill-health include:

- Panic attacks
- Bipolar disorder
- Body dysmorphic disorder
- Dissociation and dissociative disorders
- Eating disorders
- Schizophrenia
- Borderline Personality disorder
- Addictive behaviours
- Post Traumatic Stress Disorder {PTSD}

Signs and symptoms of mental ill-health include:

- Feeling sad or down most of the time / days
- Confused thinking or reduced ability to concentrate

- Excessive fears or worries, or extreme feelings of guilt
- Extreme mood changes of highs and lows
- Withdrawal from friends and activities
- Significant tiredness, low energy or problems sleeping
- Detachment from reality (delusions), paranoia or hallucinations
- Inability to cope with daily problems or stress
- Trouble understanding and relating to situations and to people
- Problem with alcohol or drug use
- Major changes in eating habits
- Excessive anger, hostility or violence
- Suicidal thinking

Can mental ill-health be treated?

The answer here is a definite 'Yes'. Mental ill-health is treatable, and most people with mental health issues do recover to live a productive and happy lives.

The first step in the treatment process is to see your doctor. Your doctor can prescribe some medications depending on the severity of your condition. He can also refer you to some psychological therapies depending on what will be suitable for you. Or to a mental health worker who can explore and help you change your lifestyle, or apply some complementary therapies such as relaxation strategies.

You can also seek for help with a private therapist if you can afford it.

I will recommend **betterHelp.com** for those who are happy with online video or phone calls and messaging. This is a very good service for couples, individuals and teens. Thanks to COVID lockdown, this has become the most popular and very helpful service.

Another good service can be found at **counselling-directory.org.uk**. Here you can search for a qualified counsellor or therapist close to where you live and can visit for face-to-face sessions if you prefer this way of working.

You can also do the following to boost your mental health:
- Take advantage of the support of your family, friends and your community
- Have a strong sense of your identity and culture, visit the country of your origin if you were born and reside abroad

- Look after your physical health by eating a healthy diet and exercising
- Reduce stress by whatever means. Ongoing stress is the main cause of escalated mental ill-health in the West.
- Be optimistic, learn to look at the good side of things. Think positive.
- Develop ways of coping with life stresses; your personal resources and self-care. Rest when you need to. Have and engage regularly in hobbies that make you feel happy and relaxed; these will give you breaks from stressful living.
- Get help when you need it.

Chapter 9

The Most Important Relationship

The beauty of this relationship is that you have the freedom to intentionally enter into it. And it can undo whatever emotional, mental and / or spiritual damage you have experienced in your life. This relationship can heal all your brokenness, woundedness and traumas, and release you into living your life with hope, meaning and purpose, and be fulfilled.

I guessed by now you are wondering what kind of relationship I'm talking about. Well, here it is: the God and human relationship. Now, don't put this book down if you do not believe in God. Just read on because you need to hear the full story, and then made up your mind based on being fully informed.

Or if you are thinking, 'Is a relationship with God possible? Keep on reading for you are about to find out the answer that you need.

How about if you feel you already know God but you are still struggling emotionally or mentally? Still keep on reading. Your mind may be enlightened more at the end and you will be able to resolve the puzzles of your life.

Here goes the story:

Once upon a time:

'When the cool evening breezes were blowing, the man and his wife heard the Lord God walking about in the garden. So, they hid from the Lord God among the trees. Then the Lord God called to the man, 'Where are you?' The man replied, 'I heard you walking in the garden, so I hid. I was afraid because I was naked' (Genesis 3: 8 – 10)

Background information: Once the Lord God created the heaven and earth and everything in it that we can see with our physical eyes and things that we cannot see with our physical eyes. In an exclusive spot on the earth, he created a beautiful garden and furnished it with all things that can make life beautiful, relaxing and enjoyable. He then created the man and the woman in his likeness to live in this beautiful garden and entrusted his creation into their care. He loved this couple so much and used to visit them at the end of their day just to enjoy their company as they chatted to him about their day. He created them for relationship with himself.

On earth also was a created spirit being, the devil, who had rebelled against the Lord God. He used to be a beautiful angel until he became prideful and rebelled taking with him some of the angels, now demons. The devil became jealous of the love relationship between the Lord God and the couple. One day, as the woman was going about her normal duty of tending the flowers, the devil got into a serpent, and went for a chat with the woman. The woman was used to talking with all the animals in the garden and so engaged in the chat innocently. The chat went like this:

Serpent: Hello! How are you doing?

The woman: Hello! I'm good! (Smiling)

Serpent: I see! You are only picking flowers! Did God say you must not eat the fruit from any of the trees in the garden?

The woman (laughing): Of course we may eat fruits from the trees in the garden. It is only the fruit from the tree in the middle of the garden that we are not allowed to eat. God said, 'You must not eat or even touch it; if you do, you will die.'

The serpent (slithered closed to the woman's ears: You won't die! God knows that your eyes will be opened as soon as you eat it, and you will be like God, knowing both good and evil'

The serpent left after this conversation with a glee.

The woman reflected on the conversation. She began to wonder if God was hiding something from them by telling them not to eat from that particular tree. Eventually, she became convinced. She advanced towards the tree and touched it. Nothing happened to her surprise. She reached out and plucked up one of the fruits that was very beautiful and look juicy and bit into it. Again, to her surprise, nothing happened. She then gave the fruit to her husband and convinced him to eat; it was very tasty. However, as soon as the man bit into the fruit, their eyes were open, they lost their innocence. They became aware of their nakedness and were ashamed. They stitched some leaves together and cover themselves. You can imagine what a poor covering that was.

That evening, when the Lord God came to visit as usual, something was terribly wrong; the couple ran and hid themselves. God's heart was broken. In anguish, he called out to the man, 'Where are you?'. The response from the man was a very sad one indeed as he confesses hiding because he was naked, ashamed, guilty and afraid.

This began the roller coaster of man's self-awareness because of his wrong desires for knowledge, and the shame, the guilt and the fear that comes with it.

Did this deter God from loving the humans that he created? Not at all! If you read down that chapter, verse 21 says,

> 'And the Lord God made clothing from animal skins for Adam and his wife'

How loving and kind God is! He made cloths to cover their nakedness (shame, fear and guilt).

Although Adam and his wife still had to face the consequences of their sin, that is, losing their garden and the good life in it, they were covered and safe.

Safe?

You may think! Safe from what?

If you read from the beginning of that Genesis chapter 3, you will understand that the serpent, the devil who deceived them had a plan. You may ask, 'And what could have possibly been his plan?'

In the Gospel of John 10:10a, Jesus exposed the plan of the devil. He said,

> 'The thief comes only to steal, kill and destroy;'

The devil, by deceiving Eve and Adam did succeed in stealing their heart from God. His next plan was to kill and destroy them through their shame, fear and guilt but God stepped in to cloth and protect them.

The devil's plan is still the same today. First, he entices people to do their own thing and disregard God's ways which is for their protection and safety. Once, human's yield to the devil's temptations and commit the sin, he then has access into their lives to carry out his destructive plans.

God, because of his love for his creation, kick started a plan for the redemption of humans. In the same book of Genesis, chapter 3 verses 14 and 15, it says,

> 'Then the Lord God said to the serpent, 'Because you have done this (deceived this woman and man), you are cursed………You will crawl on your belly, grovelling in the dust as long as you live. And I will cause hostility between you and the woman, and between your offspring and her offspring. He will strike your head, and you will strike his heel.'

This plan of God is confirmed in Galatians 4: 4 – 7, it says,

> But when the right time came, God sent his Son, born of a woman, subject to the law. God sent him to buy freedom

for us who were slaves to the law, so that he could adopt us as his very own children. And because we are his children, God has sent the Spirit of his Son into our hearts, prompting us to call out, 'Abba, Father.' Now, you are no longer a slave but God's own child. And since you are his child, God has made you, his heir.'

The Son of God mentioned in above scripture is Jesus Christ of Nazareth. God sent him into the world through the virgin birth over 2000 years ago. He lived and walk on this earth for 33 years. In the last 3 years of his earthly life, he did amazing miracles; setting people free from their sins, healing the sick, raising the dead and demonstrated God's love to humans through his life and teachings. He willingly laid down his life on the Roman's cross for the redemption of humans. Because only Jesus' blood can cleanse human's conscience from shame, guilt and fear (the root of all emotional and mental distress). He was buried and after 3 days resurrected and is still alive today. Anyone who willingly chose to accept his love today and enter into a relationship with him would be saved and transformed.

I am one of those he saved, redeemed and delivered through his blood, and my life has been transformed. At the age of 26, I was living life my own way, doing what I want though I know it was not right. Well, most of the people around me were living the same way. The issue with me is that I was very religious. I went to church regularly and took part in every church activity that I like. However, I was living in fornication with my boyfriend. One day, I met an evangelist who challenged me with this scripture:

1 John 3:4 – 10

All who indulge in a sinful life are dangerously lawless, for sin is a major disruption of God's order. Surely you know that Christ showed up in order to get rid of sin. There is no sin in him, and sin is not part of his program. No one who lives deeply in Christ makes a practice of sin. None of those who do practice sin have taken a good look at Christ. They've got him all backward.

So, my dear children, don't let anyone divert you from the truth. It's the person who acts right that is right, just as we see it lived out in our righteous Messiah. Those who make a practice of sin are straight from the Devil, the pioneer in the practice of sin. The Son of God entered the scene to abolish the Devil's ways.

People conceived and brought into life by God don't make a practice of sin. How could they? God's seed is deep within them, making them who they are. It's not the nature of the God-born to practice and parade sin. Here's how you tell the difference between God's children and the Devil's children. The one who won't practice righteous ways isn't from God, nor is the one who won't love brother or sister. A simple test (The Message Translation).

I was convicted by these words. I repented from my sins and accepted his forgiveness and love. I literally felt the weight of sin lifted of my life when the evangelist prayed with me. I was filled with incredible peace and joy. That marked the onset of my relationship with God that led me to know who I am as I continued in studying his word daily, in prayer and in fellowship with the church family wherever I am. I am who I am today because of this relationship. I got to know my identity and true purpose in life through this relationship.

I am not the only one though. There are numerous people who got to know God through Jesus Christ whose lives have also been transformed.

I would mention a popular Bible teacher here because she does not hide her testimony, she tells it on the Television all over the world. Her name is Joyce Meyer. Her television programme is called 'Enjoying Every Day Life'. You need to hear her story if you have not already. Sexually abused by her father and abandoned by her mother, she could have been a hopeless case. However, with her relationship with God, she has been transformed and is living her life with purpose, meaning, feeling fulfilled and being a great blessing to the whole world.

This is what this relationship with God will do for anyone who chose to enter into it. God can heal all the wounds in your life through the traumas and adversities that you have gone through. He can restore your life to be what he created you to be and to live as he created you to live: blessed and a blessing to your world.

'Everyone is looking for three things in life: Love, Purpose and Community' Nicky Gumble # Amsterdam2023

In God, all these needs are met. His love is unconditional, safe, affirming and secure. In getting to know him. We get to know our identity and purpose in life. The reason why we are here on earth. And as we engage with his purpose and plans for our lives, and in the community, he has placed us in (the church), we will thrive, be blessed and become a blessing to those in our sphere of influence. This is the whole essence of life and living.

My encouragement to the reader now is:

If you believe in God and are still experiencing some hurts in your life, or living life without purpose and fulfilment, ask him to show you and direct you to his plan of healing and restoration for you. God's plan is for you to live life in abundance. He has a plan and purpose for you. Don't just drift through life.

I have been a born-again Christian for 14 years before I felt the Lord's leading into counselling. He directed me to start with some counselling trainings that incorporated personal therapy. This brought me to a place of deep healing and freedom from deep childhood issues of fear and anxieties that I was not aware of previously. God wants us to live life fully and enjoy ourselves as we walk in a relationship with him.

If you are not in a relationship with God, thank you for reading so far. I supposed you are convinced and would like to begin this journey. If this is the case, then pray this prayer:

Father God, thank you for loving me and showing your love by sending Jesus to die for my sins. I'm sorry for my sins. Today, I repent and give you my heart and life. Please, forgive me. Jesus, please wash me with your blood and fill me with your Spirit. I receive you as my Saviour and Lord. Please take my life and do something with it. Thank you!

Congratulations if you have prayed this prayer from your heart. You have now become a child of God.

The next thing you need to do is get a Bible and begin to read from the New Testament daily. This will help you develop your relationship with Jesus. He is the Living Word. Make a habit of journaling what he is saying to you through the Bible and communicate with him as with a friend. Be open in talking to him about your heart issues. He is the best friend that you can ever have. Ask him to show you the right church to attend so you can become part of God's family on earth.

I will recommend you follow these ministries: God TV, Kenneth Copeland or Joyce Meyer. They can help you grow and develop in your faith and in your relationship with God. You can find them on the web, via Google or on You Tube

Finally, I would say, 'Enjoy your relationship with your Heavenly Father! He is a very good Father. You will get to experience his goodness daily as you walk and talk with his Holy Spirit that is in you.

Be aware, Your Spiritual Life is indispensable!

To live life with meaning, purpose and be fulfilled, we, as humans need a balance with our Spiritual, Mental and Emotional lives. Our physical and social lives is a reflection of our Spiritual, Mental and Emotional lives.

Chapter 10

Self Help Tips

Here's some things you can do to help you regulate and expand your mental and emotional health. This is based on your self-awareness, that is your ability to understand what is going on in the inside of you.

1. **A simple breathing exercise can help with anxiety, panics, fears, anger, frustration, worries and phobias.**

When you feel this emotion rising up in your inside, leave the site that provokes the emotion (for example, you are having a heated argument with a family member or at the office, and find some anger rising in your chest, just chose to walk away). Find a quiet place; sometimes the best quiet place may be the toilet. Sit down, close your eyes if you want to, straighten your spine, take in a deep breath through your nose, open your mouth and breath it out. As you breath out, imagine you are breathing out this emotion that has risen into your chest. Keep repeating the breathing exercise until you feel calm. Then you can go out and confront the situation that provokes it if you want to without the negative emotion interfering with your communication. You will may be able to resolve the issue. However, this will also depend on those involve being able to self-regulate.

If you are unable to calm yourself down with this simple breathing exercise, this will be an indication you need the help of a counsellor or therapist. Please, don't shy away from reaching out because you deserve to be happy.

2. **Journaling your thoughts and feelings: You can walk through your pains and hurts by this simple exercise.**

   This is how to do it: When ongoing thoughts keep troubling you and provoking negative emotions, just pick a paper and pen (I do not recommend writing these in a diary, you would soon know the reason).

Write out these thoughts preferably in a printing paper, or a paper that you do not need to keep. In the process of writing these out, imagine you are emptying these thoughts from your mind onto the paper. When you have finished, you can then rip it up and through it into a bin with an attitude that you do not want to keep it. You can now practice the above breathing exercise to help you self-regulate.

3. Anger is one of the emotion many people try to suppress. Let me tell you, this is not healthy for you. Anger is a good emotion. It tells you something is not right and need to be address. However, trying to address the situation while you are still angry will also mess it up. So, what do you do? Here's my recommendation: You first need to release the anger from your system. If you are suppressing it, it will come out in another situation that is totally not related to the cause of the anger. Or worse, you would turn it into yourself. When anger is continually suppressed and for a long time, it turns into anxiety and depression. This I experienced from my work. Most of my clients came with anxiety and depression, but in the process of working through these, they will get in touch with the anger they had experienced in some adverse events in their lives but suppressed it, either because they did not know how to release it or were too afraid to release it. As they are

supported to release this anger in a safe way, they experienced freedom.

It is important that anger is released in a safe way. Unsafe release of anger hurts those we love especially our children, partners and family members. The outcome can be a generational trauma if not dealt with.

Here are safe ways to release anger:
- The breathing exercise above can help.
- Boxing exercise is a good one; you can box your pillows or cushions or any soft material. This way you can release the anger from your system without hurting yourself.
- Going out for a walk and combining this with the breathing exercise is a good way.
- Working out at the gym
- Screaming out; this may surprise you but it's actually a very good way to release anger from your system. It is not good though if you scream at people. I recommend screaming in your shower, into the air, at open spaces like the park, at trees or at anything safe.

4. Panic is when our brain responds to a sudden event that is threatening. It can be actual or in the past. We respond in various ways to the threat; fight,

flight or frozen. This means, some people will fight the threat, some will run away from the threat and some will just stand still, not knowing what to do or waiting for the threat to go away.

What can help if and when you experience panic is grounding yourself;

The breathing exercise above can be very helpful in self-grounding. While in this mood, you can also intentionally, observe the environment that you are in noting what you can see, hear, smell and taste. You can count how many things you can see, hear, smell and taste. Just by simply becoming aware of your environment can help you depict if it is safe or not, self-regulate and take a decisive action.

Note, above are just tips to help you self-regulate your thoughts and emotions. However, these emotions may be rooted in what you belief about yourself, others and your environment / community. So, if you do not find these tips helpful, this may be an indication you need further help. Please do not hesitate to reach out for the needed help, because, as I have said before, you deserve to be happy. This is a choice only you can make for your own benefit. And making this right choice will go a long way to improve your relationship with your loved ones. The ripple effect of this will be a better future for the rest of your generation as you chose to break the curse of generational mental ill-health.

I recommend the following sites for counselling and therapeutic work:

- BetterHelp.com
- Counselling-directory.org.uk
- Or just google your local counsellor / therapist if you prefer face to face sessions.

NHS England advocate these five steps that you can also take to improve your mental health:

- 1. Connect with other people

Building and maintaining strong social connections with family, friends, colleagues and neighbours is vital for wellbeing.

- 2. Be physically active

Engaging in physical activities, no matter how small, can significantly boost mood, energy levels, and overall wellbeing.

- 3. Learn new skills

Developing new skills, trying new things, or expanding your knowledge can boost self-confidence and enhance your sense of purpose.

- 4. Give to others

Helping others, volunteering, or simply being kind can create a sense of purpose and improve your emotional well-being.

- 5. Pay attention to the present moment (mindfulness)

Being present and fully engaged with whatever you are doing at the moment – free from distraction or judgement, and aware of your thoughts and feelings without being flooded with them is good for mental health.

The breathing exercises described on Page 65 – Self Help Tips can help you in practising mindfulness.

Conclusion

Thank you for reading this book. I hope as you come to this last page, you have gained some awareness or understand something you did not understood before about Mental illness. And that this understanding will enhance your life in a positive way and the lives of those around you.

Note, you have to act on your awareness and understanding by taking the necessary steps to reach out for help if you need to, or encourage your loved ones to reach out if they need to. There is nothing to be ashamed of with mental illness. It just needs to be healed just like some physical illnesses.

Be aware; Your Mental Health is Your Wealth!!!

Personal Reflection

Thank you so much for reading this book to the end.

Now, I want to encourage you to take time to reflect on these

Questions:

Who am I, really?

What worries me most about the future?

If these were the last days of my life, how would I like to live daily?

What am I really afraid of?

Am I holding on to something I need to let go?

What matters most in my life now?

Who really matters in my life now?

What decision do I need to make to change my life?

If not now, then when?

Who do I need to bless today?

What am I thankful for in my life?

Practice 5 minutes thankfulness when you wake up.

What problem can I help solve today?

What drains me?

What inspires or energies me?

Focus more on these things.

What is it like to be me?

What makes me uncomfortable?

What makes me angry?

practice good anger management.

What are my strength and resources?

What are my weaknesses?

What makes me happy?

Do these things daily.

What makes me sad?

It's okay to mourn your losses.

How can I influence my family for good?

How can I make a difference in my community?

How can I make a difference in my country / nation?

How can I make a difference in this world?

What legacy do I want to leave for my family?

Useful quotes:

Be who you are not who the world wants you to be!

In life our only limits are the ones we give ourselves!

Don't just go through life! Learn through life!

Live life fully and make a difference!

Love is what makes the world a better place. Learn to love sincerely!

Be kind and patient with yourself and with others!

Positive thinking leads to positive life!

Negative thinking spiral into negative life!

Everyone has the freedom of choice, but no one is free from the consequences of their choices!

You can choose to use your life for good or for evil!

It's okay:

- To make mistakes. This is how we learn from our experiences!

- Not be okay

- Have hard days / challenges in life! They made you strong!

- Be yourself and not apology for it!

- To accept that Everyone is different!

- Not know it all - accept your limitations!

- Ask for and receive help!

- Fail and start over again!

- Need and give yourself more time!

Acknowledgement

I'm grateful to all my clients for this work. They have been my source of inspiration and motivation. Knowing each of these precious ones has greatly enhance my life; give me purpose, passion and fulfilment in doing this work. I am truly thankful.

The information in this book comes from my personal and work experiences, professional trainings and development, and research from Google.

Images are from Online Unknown Authors licenced under CC BY-NC-ND-SA

Scriptural quotes are from the New Living Translation Bible, unless mentioned otherwise.

Author's page

Susan Abraham is a professional counsellor.

Her previous career was as a Registered Adult Nurse.

While working as a Registered Nurse, she had a poster came through her letter box advertising Level 2 Counselling Skills in her local college. She was curious and registered for the course. This marked a turning point in her life at the age of 40. She got to love this counselling course so much that she continued in to Level 3, progressed into Level 4 & 5 Diploma in Integrative Counselling and Graduate Certificate in Couple and family therapy.

In 2010, she started her Private Practice which was flourishing until COVID isolation brought that to a standstill. Prior to this, she was also doing part time work in General Practices. Currently, she works in General Practices and with the NHS.

She works with varieties of mental health problems; anxiety, depression, bereavement, addictions, relationship problems, traumas, low self-esteem / confidence, panic attacks, stress etc.

Susan sees mental illness as poor relationship with self. Every child is perfect at birth. However, in the process of growing up, we get to encounter various adversities, traumas and environmental factors that caused some brokenness and result in griefs. These hinders our ability to self-regulate; in other words, relate well with ourselves, be ourselves and live authentically. Subsequently, this impact on our relationship with others.

Susan aim in her work is to see broken lives healed and restored. Subsequently, these individuals will move on to live authentically, find their purpose in life, be passionate with their purpose, live fulfilled and be happy.

The reason Susan wrote this book is to help the ordinary person understand mental illness and to know everyone with mental illness can be heal, and can have a normal life again. She hopes the reader will be inspired accordingly.

Susan is an author of another book called Life with God. The Most Exciting Adventure. It's a true-life fiction, exciting and inspirational. A must read! You can find it on amazon.co.uk

For more information or questions, you can contact Susan via this email:

acps.ad@gmail.com

Words associated with mental health / ill-health

Emotion

Mind

Feelings

Anxiety

Sadness

Anger

Depression

Neurodiversity

Emotional distress

Trauma

Mental health challenges

Bipolar

Post traumatic stress disorder (ptsd)

Schizophrenia and psychosis

Eating disorders

Adha

autism

Neurodevelopmental disorders

Disruptive behaviour dissocial disorders

Paranoia

Obsessive compulsive disorder (ocd)

Borderline personality disorder

You can use the following pages to record your self-awareness / reflections while reading this book, and the action/s that you are going to take to change / improve your life and your relationships.

Printed in Dunstable, United Kingdom